Domestic Recusals

Simon Constam

AOS Publishing, 2024

Copyright © 2024

Simon Constam

All rights reserved under International
and Pan-American copyright conventions

ISBN: 978-1-990496-47-9

Cover Design: Jessica James

Visit AOS Publishing's website:
www.aospublishing.com

A Better Wife

Someone who dined alone tonight,
dreamed a wife who had not died,
dreamed a better wife.

It was a moment he did not want to hold onto,
the phrase embarrassed him – a better wife.
He turned away to try to hear
a different voice within himself.

But at the visitation, he told her closest friend,
"She could be picky." It was an insignificant accusation
that both of them understood to be less than what he meant.
"I don't remember her that way," she had replied.

"They were late," he said, "serving the secondo and contorno
the night she died. She had no patience for delay,
and on this occasion, she was particularly angry.
It didn't kill her of course, but the doctors said
it might have been a factor."

At home, in the silence of his home, *a better wife*,
the words came back to him.
"What can I possibly have meant by that?" he said aloud.
"Why did I have this thought today and why
do I have it again now?" She could be picky.
She could be ill-tempered. She was impatient
in many things: in bank lineups, in parking lots,
when the children were still young, and also
oftentimes in bed.
But now he's told his wife's best friend
and it will be remarked upon
in several houses before the week is out.

All his married life he scarcely noticed faults in her
that now he seemed incapable of not revealing
to himself. And if he felt she hovered nearby still,
he thought the revelation must somehow also be
her doing. This is what you really felt about me,
she was saying. I wish you'd had more courage.
I wish that you'd been stronger.

He wished the same himself.
He wished he could think of her passing
as his loss of heaven.
But he knew the truth and dreaded it,
he wished he'd had a better wife.

Pentimento

I've been thinking about what it is not to love.
Not to love the stranger standing in front of you.
Not to love the one you're with.
Not to love the one that you abandoned.
Not to love the unlived story that you can't fathom or forget.
How cruel not to be able to love enough of what has happened.
Not to love the gray deserted road your turn to face
and not to love what might never come to be.

If I were a painter

If I were a painter,
I'd paint your face onto a cat.
I'd paint the cat onto a sofa.
I'd paint the sofa into a large sitting room.
I'd paint the sitting-room into a fine old house.
I'd paint the house into a forest.
The forest is dark and deep.

Remorse gripped me.

I walked on for hours in the darkness,
I lay down on a bed of ferns.

I awoke in the middle of the night,
your fate overwhelmed me.

I walked on through the night,
I found the house.

The light behind its windows was saffron,
I saw a figure moving but it was not you.

I need to be found, you told me
 but I was frightened,

I hid shivering in the forest all day long.

I saw through the window that you were quite happy
in front of the fire smiling while they watched you.

O, I am a painter, I have stolen faces
and lives and taken strangers down
tortuous pathways into beings they are not.
I have traduced many souls with my art.

I have forgiven myself a thousand times.
I have dreamt that I could paint you
out of that house
and away from the cat,
and back into my arms.

But you say no.
You stay in the forest.
You stayed in the forest.
I forsook my powers
but you stayed in the forest.
I begged you.

Quietly, I begged you.

Now, finally, I hear behind my arrogance
my failure,
 Art has misled me.
The tension between
my talent
and my ambition to love
has destroyed me.

The Theatre of Us

When I go to bed, sometimes I have to pause
just inside the doorway, so my eyes can register
what lies before me in the darkness and not mistake
this house for another I used to know.

Beneath the covers, my hand searches for her bare skin.
Finding it, I unlock a quiet reverie.
I remember we were alone beside the river,
on a warm evening. Were there people nearby?
We had just climbed up the riverbank after a dip.

Perhaps the children told their parents that they had seen
a man and woman naked.
Someone at any rate is resolving the images in their mind
and clarifying the meaning of them.
For every image there's a clairvoyant who is charged with
record-keeping and a clairaudient to get the poetry.

Marjorie and I are a bit befuddled by it all, sitting now
unrecognized in the darkened theatre, embarrassed
that a small bit of ourselves has been found out
and used as a life lesson for their children.

Love

Love, as when in an innocent moment,
she touches my shoulder.
Love, the excruciating gentleness of it.
Love, as when you settle for a love that isn't dramatic.
Love, as when whatever it offers, you accept.

Beauty

Her skin is shivering.
Her breasts are young again.
Her head has fallen against my shoulder.
I have wanted to be this close to her.
Suddenly, I realize I must stop trying to
always to make something beautiful
when it requires, in the moment
and in the memory of it,
nothing.

Passage

In the rooms of our house though she no longer appears,

her presence to a greater degree or lesser

is a thing some instrument in me recognizes.

She has affixed herself to me. She moves around the room

in images. Our furniture, modern midcentury,

her fair-trade tchotchkes and the flowers in their bud

and cube vases are dispositive. As they always have,

they bend toward her.

Six months, they tell me, before she disappears entirely.

It happens slowly, room by room. She doesn't
entirely want to go. This both torments and comforts me.
Nor does Time want to let go of everything calmly.
Friday nights, in particular, won't let go of her.

Some objects might hold her here for years on end.
Who knows? Some narrow passages between and around
sofa and chairs, two-step movements between rooms,
singing, may never release her.

It takes more than one effort to abandon a lover –
a ferocious will, a conspiracy to forget, a desire to live,
a final understanding
of there being no alternative.

Looking Intently on What is Hidden

When I do not tell her that I love her,
I am withholding my love.
When I do not tell her that I love her,
I deny that within me which seeks to love the world.
When I do not tell her that I love her,
I feel strong and cruel.
When I do not tell her that I love her,
I twist her voice into silence.
I silence the world.

Divorce

One recognizes the themes of one's life
shortly after one's fourth or fifth decade.
So it was in my case, my story had
decayed with its patterned repetitions
of my unhappy ways.

Love's a locket.
Love is a letter of intent,
an heirloom from an earlier age,
a photograph,
the way a touch betrays.

I left in the lull of an argument when the
lawyers paused for a smoke and a drink.

I learned to leave when the lights are dimmed
by the mind's inability to fill them in.
I learned to leave at just the right moment
to be insensate in the easiest way.

The Precision of Sadness

When in the late evening she coughs
and I do not turn to look at her,
and I do not think to bring her water,
it bothers her.

And when in the hour I drowse
I forgive myself all I've done.
And there, in the next room she pauses
and it occurs to me again that I am selfish.

I think of the forest of years that has surrounded us,
the undergrowth that everything becomes,
the canopy that closes the summer light away
the separate holiness that sometimes pleases us.

But one day she looks at me and says,
"Perhaps the way out of this loneliness
is to look more closely at each other."
It's just a thought, she says.

Over many years my thoughts turn both ways,
toward her and away abruptly.
No set of circumstances are
dependable to what causes love or its opposite.

She thinks she knows precisely what she wants now,
a close but not too close reading of love,
separate bedrooms, separate bathrooms.

I am thinking that perhaps I just ought to leave.
That's the thought that I revolve around,
some distant place where I would be found
in a library on an afternoon by a woman
who is a beautiful, a calm household
firmly etched in her mind.

The Beauty of her Imperfection

Beneath the shower,
sitting slumped
against the white tile wall,
she is confused, subdued,
hair tied on top of her head
but some strands
have fallen.

It's all too much for me.
I resent being the one
called upon to pull her up
from despair.

She overhears that thought...

She says she doesn't want
that anyway and asks me
to come down below to her
instead.

Inflammatory

I've been thinking tonight
about the last narrow space
between two people,
how it never closes completely.

The crack where the darkness enters,
think of all the silence that small passage
has engendered. Think of all the efforts
made to tell us it doesn't even exist,
or if it does, how it can be made to disappear.

Think of the magnitudes of love
that grow when it is accepted.

The Idea of Sex

The idea of sex fades away,
not just in age but
in a passing hour.
Fragile as a flower set on fire.
Argument has no power and prayers
are as useless as hunger.

There is no image to retreat to.
No memory but its odd contortions.
No scaffold of fantasy to repeat.
No medicine for this disease.

I don't know
or I have forgotten
how it happened,

She was asleep in the bedroom.
"What in the world will I do," I said to myself,
"when she wakes?"

Rich in the Moment

She takes an angry nap before our evening walk,
having left me with a vision of myself destitute,
5 years from now or 10.

I manage it quite easily, a mob of thoughts
as if it were a book I cannot bring myself
to ever depart from.

How easily I look away, deny a thought.
I've put my mind at ease over all those wars abroad.
I do not need to contemplate disaster.
So many things I keep at a distance from myself.
I can hold up my hand to occlude a sunset,
wipe out the full moon and even can deny
the enormity of a black map full of stars.
And how easy to smuggle an idea
into the memory palace that holds
a lifetime of dreams gone wrong and scars.

Still, it wanders close and when she finally awakes,
I have already been living in the rundown neighbourhood
for several years. Most months I barely make the rent.
I'm happy to keep people away from me and make
young naked friends on the internet instead.

We walk out into the evening dream of trees
and breezes and crowds of lovers.
It makes me put my arm around her waist.
The city streets are full of us, the bien-pensants.

Besides, I don't find hope in remonstrance.
I have told her none of this. I let it slip away.
I should not exacerbate the tensions between us.
It's almost been a perfect day.

The End of a Small History

I cannot remember who I once was.
She looks at me repeatedly thinking,
I'm sure, that I remember every moment of pain,
as does she.

Memory's argument is simply this. You do not
remember how badly you hurt me.

It arrives on a sullen, snowy winter's night.
The stillness of the moment only remembers
the pain not the arguments, not the choreography.

Once again, an argument that intends to leave unsettled.
I will not try to hold it back from leaving.

I cannot remember who I once was
and she looks at me repeatedly again.

Distance comes between us claiming its measure is true.
The cold night air believes it.

And it draws attention to another love
long passed and another far away and a third

just down the street thoroughly unearned.
The sense of pleasure lost, on this night

is early on assumed. And as expected,
the finely tuned world closes its history
as written.

I Know a Woman

I love her down to her inmost thoughts,
down to the screws, down to the parts made for her,
even the places where the seams are revealed.

I love the parts not born in her mother's milk,
the parts she made for herself,
and all the do-not-fall-apart workarounds
made out of all her weaknesses turned into strengths,
and even those weaknesses that still hold fast.

I love the places where the other voices appear,
the incidents that drain her courage away,
and those that quietly assure her. I love her beingness,
made out of not-words, windows covered,
blinds drawn, sounds muffled, enveloped in darkness.

She is made of evening promises,
long conversations of profound stillness,
and morning fits of anger
like clothes she otherwise never wears.
The indefinable sadness so naturally affinitied
with death the older she becomes.

I love her quiet after breakfast,
her surprise that much that should have changed has not.
I love the things she can call on for softness
and the outrage that stirs her against
what conspires on earth against us.
I love the way she analyzes our relationship.
I love the way she changes.

Overwinter

You left today, leaving behind a note,
a drop of you, a concentrate.

You'll spend some time up north.
"Better to be happy this way, missing you,"

you wrote, "than hear you say
I love you (as if you're quoting someone).

And one month or even two may not be enough.
A friend I know who owns a cabin right on Rock Lake
has gone away. I can stay as long as it moves me to.

I'd like to see the winter out
up here, at least. I've taken food enough
and books. But I know you'll worry.
I'll be okay.

I'll take care of myself.
I've been behaving badly toward you.
I need to think on that."

I've known her long enough.
I doubt I'll think too much
on what she's doing

or whether anyone else
will take some time with her.
I think I can be quiet now.

And calm. And even happy
to have not loved too much.

Old Friends

together again
and because it is
the most inappropriate thing
that either of them can imagine,
they fuck.
It is a glorious mess.
exquisite, fulfilling, impious, anfractuous,
ontological, anagogical, agathokakological,
tenebrific, weird, solipsistic.

Wonderful!

Full of weltschmerz, rebellion, paranoia, resurrection.
All of my identity changed and unchanged, the paradox
of relationships while not escaping from being alone,
completely.

And, may I say, both of them, are quite prepared
if cross-examined,
to regret this happiness,
which, nevertheless
they know
will be
unrivalled in
all the long rest
of their lives.

Orrery

If I go outside and it happens to be
a cold, clear night,
I take an hour there.
But I still damn the cover of dirty light
that obscures the stars.

And then I say nothing when I'm back inside.
Everyone is sitting around watching football.
No one asks me where I've been.
My bride is feigning interest in the game
giving me the stare when I pass between
our guests and the 60-inch television.

Time is wasting away.
She is going to be beautiful for only so long.
That's true, isn't it?
I think you know what I mean.
Love thinks time is obscene.

As like as not, I know what love is.
She enters and leaves. I don't know
enough of what she thinks of me.
We never mention it, and I am and she's
holding too fast to the idea we brought with us.
and even though it's a neutral darkness,
it's still the kind you can't be saved from.

And then they're gone.
And she turns to me
sympathetic, and yes
of all the versions of her,
the one that softens into love
is unclear tonight.
She has it, I assume, at her fingertips
but perhaps not. She goes upstairs.
I'd follow but she hasn't asked me too
so I pause at the window by the back door
to imagine the planets in their places
revolving at the speed they've been given
seeming to move closer to one another,
as often as not, appearing to
have absolutely nothing to do with each other.

About Beauty

I can only go so far with beauty.
I have agreed not to look too deeply
to avoid the temptations of entanglement
that only prayer can rectify.

Beauty in all its fullness, vividity,
the quiet and the exaggeration of it
taunts me. It is the way the world
wants to tie itself to me.
It is too much. It overwhelms.

It preoccupies.
It thinks too highly of itself.
It consumes too much praise,
bloats, becomes amorphous.

It blots out the sun.
It is not the whole truth.
It will not say what is behind it.
It renders one inarticulate, insensate.
It is inoperable.

It says that it will not die.
We know better.
It won't admit that it changes.
Its claim of purity is untenable.

It waylays us on the journey, deflects us
from our beautiful ordinariness too often
and for too long.

And still,
it is always just out of reach.

The surfeit of beauty overwhelms
my desire not to be ruled by it.
Think how different life would be
if breathing were not interfered with
by beauty.

Perhaps Even These Things, One Day,
Will Be Pleasing To Remember

Forsan Et Haec Olim Meminisse Iuvabit
- Virgil, Aeneid 1.203

She is a strange being in the other room, finally
coming back out here as if nothing has changed.

It is very quiet between us.
The moment is disturbed by her stillness.

She tries to hide her beauty in plain sight.
Tell no one about the distance between two lovers.

She Returns Today

She returns today from several months in Germany.
It was not nearly soon enough for me.
Spring has turned to summer here.
The changes make a world that scarcely coheres
with what has been before and also we will greet
each other without betraying or satisfying any need,
almost certainly at least in some deep regard as strangers.

On her arrival home, the spaniel eagerly
repeals his recent history with me for their selfish pleasure.
Curtains are parted, the breeze
that has hovered outside for weeks
now does not hesitate to enter.
And, as if they are her own idea, suddenly freshness and order
take precedence in everything. The corners of the bed
are made to behave lest the sight of them not tucked in
leaves her incomplete and anxious.

The bathroom scrubbed so diligently by me is checked
and re-checked, as if it is a given I have neglected
it. But more importantly, the ambition that upkeep
demands, that I abandoned in favor of rest and sleep
has returned as surely as if it was another person
who does not need to speak such clearly obvious lessons
and also happily assesses an irreducible blame.

At times like this two people cannot easily interact.
Her practiced movements in and out of tasks,
repairing places large and small that have been ruined
in her absence but which she's sure will soon be back in
something like their pristine state, lead inexorably
to her erstwhile primacy. For me though, it aggravates
the natural order that says let things fall apart and fade.

Now the sun has come to warm the window where I sit.
And even I can see how lovely sunlight is,
painting trees, the grasses and the flowers,
and catching her too in a fleeting spotlight that is now hers
alone. And now I see her in a different light
and suddenly, yes, it's true and almost certainly right,
what I feel for her will not likely ever change.

I'm loathe to give this thing I feel a name.
After all, it isn't always there. It comes and goes like rain.
I think that I shall never be completely certain but,
as if there is such a thing as love,
we love each other once again
and all that went before, we never talk of.

To Love

She must be aware of the slow movement of my right hand
toward her left breast begun a month ago.
How could she not,
though I have tried my best to disguise it?

She must be aware. I am staring. I am inhaling.
The pheromones are trading places.
Your eyes, your voice, there really is no choice.
The swerve of love has started.

Love always has its start, and you must choose
to let it travel onwards or to end it.

Yes, it is always the figure in the distance,
the stranger in one's bed,
the stranger in one's future,
the tumult in your head.

How intense the hope and hopelessness
that strangers feel! The urge will not relent.
I believe what I have been told
about nakedness,
that it confuses the alarms
but still reveals something unspeakably lovely
to the cold moments that stand in the wings
with their patient and harmful intensities.

On any clear day
as winter starts out in the shadows,
or summer beats its breast in the heat,
when the dim lighting has no meaning,
other than to hide its lovers,
loneliness still forever threatens.

If love is a verb

If love is a verb,
it cannot be seen in a glimpse or a glance.
It cannot be seen in a photograph.
It moves too fast for the camera to catch.
But still far too slowly for the urgent need
that hungers after it.

If love is intransitive,
I dream the idea of you,
the meta of you.
The manifestation of you,
a holograph. With all
of my wounded heart
I dream of you.

If love is transitive,
you are walking away from me,
your hair is black. You are the sole
object of my compulsion. It is not just
the hurrying after you, it is also
the prospect that I might fail
to reach you.

Billet-Doux

Walking out this evening,
wrapped against the snow,
when I see
the idea of home
in the eyes of passersby.

I miss you deeply.

And when I am warm again in my rooms,
my footsteps are alone.
But I lie down with you.
Listen, the future comes calling ceaselessly.
I cannot keep even your absence
here for long.

Come to Bed with Me Tonight, Solo Traveler

It makes no matter to the world that you are far
from here tonight in Ireland on one of your jaunts
to insure you are your own person. And I am searching
to articulate the reasons for my feeling dark
and almost silent.

When you're here, I am not always content when
I look across the room toward you as the day is ending.
At such moments, I do not even know if tomorrow
I will still want to be with you.

Tonight, I do not have the freedom to imagine you
far away. I taste your absence and find it shorn of
any pleasurable compensatory emptiness.
There is no dream I wish to dream tonight,

no other life that I can conjure but the one
with you beside me. I think it is the old freedom
a lover takes or tolerates in which I can imagine myself
anywhere at all at any age

with someone else or no one. I might not even
have met you. And the reveries are only sometimes
broken by you saying as you sometimes do, so tenderly,
Come to bed with me tonight.

The Usual Sky

I was driving home from work,
bitter about the guy I sit next to,
trying to improve my state of mind
in the half-hour I had before home,
the radio off and no traffic to pay inordinate attention to.

The sky was the usual sky,
shades of and the full glare of blue.
But turning to the west, gunmetal.
and in the great distance, rose quartz.

The old trick of seeing something beautiful
up in the high clouds was not working.

This was long before I ever got to sit
staring at things and enjoying having nothing to do

I decided that I wouldn't let anything interfere
at home. I swore I'd be immune to the anger.

The truth is, I've never been exactly purposeful
about this love, or otherwise
almost ready to desert her.

It was 7.42pm precisely on a Wednesday evening.
Funny, I don't remember what season it was.

Let's say it was autumn.
She had slipped into depression.

Once, I heard a dead poet on the radio
call that condition a genetic virtue.
That such hours, long days and weeks
are more truthful than others, if you let them.

You know how the moment goes.
I reach for her and she is not there.
So beautiful, that moment is, unhappily.

The embrace that misses her, her distant voice,
the thin fingers of her hands, her brown hair thinning.

She was on the couch
in the dim light of the old television set
her mother gave her.

Anna Karenina had just killed herself again.
I know this can't be good for her.

But at least her suicides can be put down
to vicarious for now.

That is the thing about dying,
it's good to do it with someone imaginary.

It opens up the idea of sharing fear
even at the worst of times.

To A Woman

Your smile remains as it has always been
your voice still as beautiful as when it
entrusted its pleasure long ago
to thrill this young man's heart.
It still complicates and it still shames
this older man with relentless lust.

But these things are not what now I treasure.
Now it is the way your step makes
uncertain contact with the earth,
the way your dress catches at the hip before it falls to the floor.
It is how your energy gives out in love.
It is even the way you no longer care if you have been seen
awkward, naked, walking out of the shower,
not a bit of your seventy years decorated for the view of others.

I can still feel the fever raging.
I can feel the fever raging as I take my part in your dying.
It is in the things you do not do for yourself anymore
to propose that I ought to love you best.

It is the turning away from your burning.
The unselfconscious freedom that is more
than you ever expected.
It is in the imperfections of your forgiveness
and that you no longer believe that you are blessed.

Little Black Book of Scars

I want to preserve her particular nakedness.
I have a mental library of her narrow hips,
her style of breasts, the frissoned surface of her skin,
her quiet lips. her sexual pleasure, and her voice
that incorporates everywhere she's been, her first lover
and the lovers that followed after he died.
Those lonely, several, dire years.

At a whim, I have the feeling of her touch. And
I have the silence of that particular smile that she knows
elicits my cruel behaviour toward her.
Now, she looks her younger self, quick to anger,
awkward, the molecules stuck in glue,
her periodic immobile moments.

I have both women when we make love.
Sometimes I am uncertain which is which.
And I have myself as well at 22
and my older self at 47
to work with.

I have my sideways glance when she undresses
and my brazen staring at her nakedness.
She knows I am searching for something that may be lost.
Something of my own that I can no longer practice.

I have the moment we learned she miscarried.
I have her too, exactly three months later almost
ready to be completely without hope, harried,
suddenly irresponsible. So utterly unlike her.

I have the exhalation we experienced together
when our daughter was born, the exact moment
we knew she would be fine.

I have the argument we waged against each other
when I didn't come home one night
and the full text of her diatribe the day
I quit my job.

I have her the day she found out
I'd gambled away almost all of our money.

And I have a photograph of her taken
at the very moment,
I think she loved me most.

I had just delivered the commencement address.
I was walking down the aisle toward her.
As I reached her, she said something to me.
There was so much going on I didn't hear it.
But her arm gently went around my shoulders
and then and there I knew it would never last.
It was just too happy a moment.

I Cannot Say

I did not recognize her beauty
until one afternoon
many years later
in the sudden
unexpected whiteness of my age.
I lay down to rest
and she appeared to me
to tell me she had died.

She wanted to know why
She had not been
beautiful to me
that evening long ago.

I was ashamed to tell her
that I do not know.

Certainty

With certainty, we subdue the inexactitudes of God.
With certainty, praise of Him comes easily.
With certainty, no one, not even God disturbs us.
With certainty, we've won the argument
with ourselves

The Two Susans

That she broke her back some years ago has made
her nakedness much more striking. Shoulders unremittingly
tense. A ladder of hierarchical worries. A temptress
of desperate ideas that come from injury. How to this
and how to that: turn, rise, parry, thrust not.
Presentation formal. Submission out of the question
yet necessary and unbearably intense.

Her whole body is still in a cast for all purposes.
Still, for love, she is young.
Lying on the bed, she is thin,
as anxious as when she was sixteen.
I was not prepared for this.

When I first met her, the slight body beneath her clothes
was an insubstantial thought subservient
to her intellectual rigour.
That was where she lived fully.
And, in the picture she would draw of herself, for herself,
there was a full panoply of her dramatis personae among whom
she walked solipsistic in the extreme.
But she wears it well.
Achieves a certain unity overall
that succeeds in minimizing what she cannot any longer be.

Love is always a thing between four people.
The fate of the world rests on this foundation,
that bodies complicate matters.
Always difficult to unify competing interests.
Love takes the form that intensity allows it.

How terrible though where sadness cannot
be placed on the bedside table and still
there is an hour to transit
until sleep and joy.

June

June has long forgotten May,
wild heat replacing dreary rain,
wind stuck hot on the midday ground,
a heavy quiet is the order of the day.

There is no turning back there is,
nothing to turn back to, no past.
no such thing, only this quiet
absence of anything that once was.

The darkening sky believes in itself.
It knows nothing else. Thunder is its music.
First, we hear the new world, and only then
see how strange we are ourselves.

Someone Running

At this very moment someone running
from a dark and violent country,
a man whose wife is always walking behind him
imagines me exhausted by a long day
returning home to a wife who is bitter
from housework and children.

He has seen much and heard such stories
and not been able to make light of them.
He fears he may have chosen the wrong country.

When the four of us are together,
I tell my wife that I love her
but he sees her reserve.
And he suspects I work at a job
I detest each day.
That all is not well with us.

Now, stepping aside at this point,
I realize this is not about my wife.
Things go wrong between two people
for all sorts of reasons. But it is
that I have disappointed new arrivals.
It makes me think I do not do
enough with what I have.

We ingratiate ourselves
into a notion of happiness
that is ratified by all and everything around us.
The soft grass of a summer afternoon,
the agreed-upon pleasures, the lakeside picnic,
the child smarter than we ever were,
the travel, the plenitude, the restaurants,
the inexhaustible youth, the grasp we have been given
of a world made especially by parents and parents
and parents for us. The seven or eight income-positive
adventures, the small happinesses that are swept aside
by other happinesses.

But now I am trapped in my own difficulty and what I have
done to challenge the lives of others. My first thought
is to run. I can show them how easy it is to move
from one life to another.
That's a good thing, no?

Or perhaps not. People want to retain all they can
when they abandon their former lives.
In the quiet moments late at night,
in the first few days after their arrival,
she says to him,
we won't be like that, will we?
And he says no.
What if we are,
can we go back?
It is very late at night,
they have both woken
from restless sleep.
They are murmuring quietly to each other
when he says as if he is
revealing a secret to his only love.
We can't go back.

Seduced

You have to know when you're being seduced.
You have to know the suitor's tricks.
You have to know the long game.
You have to know the bait and switch.

You have to know where the tower is.
You have to get to the top.
You have to overcome your weakness.
Rest, if you need to, but you may not stop.

Love, I've been told, is also a pose
but deeper, more fatal, and better disguised.
Can anyone be trusted? Perhaps, who knows?
But we've all had our fill of nice-sounding lies.

And there's your failing eyesight,
and there's your broken heart, and
your trembling soul in the dark of the night
and the distrust you cannot withstand

You have to know where rock bottom is.
You have to know that you'd leave if you must.
You have to see clearly the world as it is
and try once again to love and to trust.

A Small Spray of Sunshine and a Deliberate Breeze

A woman does not believe me when I tell her she is beautiful.
Early one morning, returning from a girl's overnight shivaree,
stumbling about the kitchen, unwittingly
knocking pots and pans into cacophony,
trying to figure how she'll get into bed
without me being aware of her insoluble condition,
she is beautiful.

But try telling that to someone
who grew up, grew out, and grew old
objecting to the whole condescending adjectival parade.
She's 63 and still not comfortable with her putative beauty.

Now she lies beside me naked and thoroughly inebriated.
Beautiful, now? she suddenly says, sarcastically.

I panic...
I think some sort of compliment right now might stick
but I'm unsteady here, hesitant, angry, a surgeon
never before having successfully completed
this precise operation, an author about to submit
a lesser work to his publisher, a politician about to lie,
incapable of finding a solution to mollify
two electorates, alike in ferocity.

Quailing from anxiety,
I demur silently when suddenly
a small spray of sunshine and a deliberate breeze
enter the room intending to change the moment.
They could change the entire world, they say,
if they so desired. Not just you, not just
now they say but certainly your halting back-and-forths,
your painful uxorious interludes.

I don't know if that is true, I think I say.

Some acts of nature ought to be forbidden
when the moment that contradicts them,
full of bitterness and unforgiving
stands so stubborn and no one
is ready to feel beautiful.

Meta-

When you want to love a person, or is it
when you think you want to love a person,
is it like thinking that you can write a brilliant novel
and the gods will be kind to you and let you do it?

Is it like what we do with the idea of meaning
that we have to have it so we arrange our minds and passions
around the specific beauty that enables it?
Right or wrong then, about meaning, is love,
a kind of arbitrary idea that allows us
to comfort and be comforted
but not a true thing of people intertwined with one another?

Is all our poetry and love-devoted art predictive then,
not reflective?
Even if we've had to make it up.
Is love like what we imagine dying is,
something that, try as we might,
we'll ultimately stand outside of,
occasionally engaged in,
and when we die not knowing
what we're being taken in by?

Acknowledgments

This poems in this book were written over a 12-year period. During this time, I was in my sixties and then my very early seventies. The poems come from experiences in and out of marriage, in and out of depression, into and out of different ideas of how men and women operate in relationships.

Some of these poems are reflections of my experience. Some are pure invention or at least the conflation of different experiences and different imaginings. Poetry can make use of fiction as much as novels do. Some of these poems are entirely fictional. The truth of them lies in what they say and how they say it.

Thank you to my friends for their unfailing willingness to criticize and make suggestions for improvement. Among these friends are: Anita Jawary, Stephanie Pressman, Shelley Saposnick, Leonard Freeman, Kate Stadt, Katherine Gregoire, Rebecca Cross, Mark Kempf, John Scholey, Joe DaSilva, Jean Wagner Sutkiewicz, the late Stan White and my many friends in the many poetry workshops where I have presented these poems for review and criticism.

Thank you also to the many readers of my original aphorisms (published daily for more than 5 years on Instagram, under the moniker Daily Ferocity and to an email subscriber list). I have gleaned many ideas from their comments and criticisms.

I am especially grateful to my editor, Tracey Nesbitt who is also the most reliable grammarian I know.

Finally, my wife Janice Waugh, accomplished in so many areas, has been invaluable to me as a friend, critic, guide, wise old bird, and lover. I have learned from her throughout the writing of this book. Above all else, her encouragement and belief in me has been indispensable.

DOMESTIC RECUSALS is dedicated to Janice Waugh.